Carving Scrooge
and
Dicken's
"A Christmas Carol"

by Vince Squeglia

FOX BOOKS
Fox Chapel Publishing Co Inc.

Box 7948
Lancaster, PA 17604

© 1996 by Fox Chapel Publishing Company, Inc.

Publisher: Alan Giagnocavo
Project Editor: Ayleen Stellhorn
Desktop Specialist: Robert Altland, Altland Design
Cover Photography:

ISBN: 1–56523–082–5

To order your copy of this book,
please send check or money order
for $12.95 plus $2.50 shipping to:
Fox Chapel Book Orders
Box 7948
Lancaster, PA 17604–7948

Try your favorite book supplier first!

Contents

Introduction

"Stave one. Marley was dead, to begin with. There is no doubt whatever about that. The register of his burial was signed by the clergyman, the clerk, the undertaker and the chief mourner. Scrooge signed it."

I was twelve years old when I first read those dark words. I did not understand why my favorite Aunt Mary gave me such a book as a Christmas present. I was disappointed because I really was expecting that neat telescope in Carters toy store window that I had been hinting at for weeks. I never did read beyond that first chilling paragraph at the time.

It was years later when I came across the book again, lost under stacks of *National Geographic,* that I read it. Only as I read past that first dark paragraph did I realize what a real treasure Aunt Mary had given me that Christmas so long ago.

The timeless classic, of course, is Charles Dickens *A Christmas Carol,* his masterwork of the human condition as it existed in the England of the 1800s. Ever since that first reading, I have made A Christmas Carol a holiday tradition. I read it every Christmas Eve; it has never failed to uplift. Each time I peruse those familiar words I am once again inspired and awed with the true meaning of the wonder and magic of Christmas.

In my career as a commercial artist, I have turned many times to *A Christmas Carol* for inspiration for my illustrations; it worked every time. In my new-found love, wood carving, I approached the classic once more, and yes, it still inspires. It will be the theme for this project and I wish you, my fellow wood carvers, the same joy I have found in producing it.

A "ponderous" project to be sure, borrowing a word from Dickens himself, but a most rewarding one as well. This piece was designed to be a show-stopper. Something that, when completed, will be a timeless classic, the same as that which inspired it.

As a wood carver, I prefer to keep things simple, it adds to the fun. A good pattern, the proper wood and some sharp tools are all that is needed to produce a good carving.

As with any creative endeavor, the artist is the most important element, not the tools or material.

Instructions for a project are meant to point the carver in the right direction. But at the same time, the carver should stretch, pull and expand his imagination, think about what he is doing, put something of himself into the work, don't just follow. By using this interpretative approach, I assure you at completion of the project, the sense of accomplishment will fill you with satisfaction with what you created.

With this in mind, may I suggest basswood for the figures. It cuts and paints well. The base can be any of the hardwoods you prefer, keeping in mind it will be stained. The backdrop could be white pine, as we will be staining and painting it. A basic set of gouges, a few knives, one up-turned blade and one down-turned blade should do it for tools.

I leave you to it, fellow wood carvers. Happy trails. *−Vince Squeglia*

Author's Note

Before we begin the project, may I suggest a few preparatory steps that I have found helpful. Except for the five figure patterns that are to scale, the rest of the patterns shown are not to scale: the base, the backdrop, the nameplate.

With this in mind, make your decision as to what size your figures are to be at this point. They will determine the proportions of the rest of the piece. If you decide to go larger or smaller than shown, you will need to rescale the base, the backdrop and other elements accordingly so everything will be in proper scale.

The figures shown range from ten inches to eight inches high. They work out to a twenty-inch-long by nine-inch-wide base, approximately. The relief backdrop measures out twelve inches at its highest point by eleven inches long, approximately. I have found these dimensions give a pleasing overall look, not too large that it becomes cumbersome and not too small so as the carving will lose detail.

Also, I suggest cutting all the figures out on the bandsaw at the same time to help you further determine overall scale. This way you will have all of the blanks in front of you to arrange. Note the shading on the figure patterns. Careful study of this shading will greatly aid you in understanding the modeling of the figures, especially the facial expressions that are very important to this project.

A masterpiece is nothing more than many details in harmony with each other.

Scrooge
Side View Patterns

Bandsaw Cut Line

Carve Line

Scrooge
Facial Expression

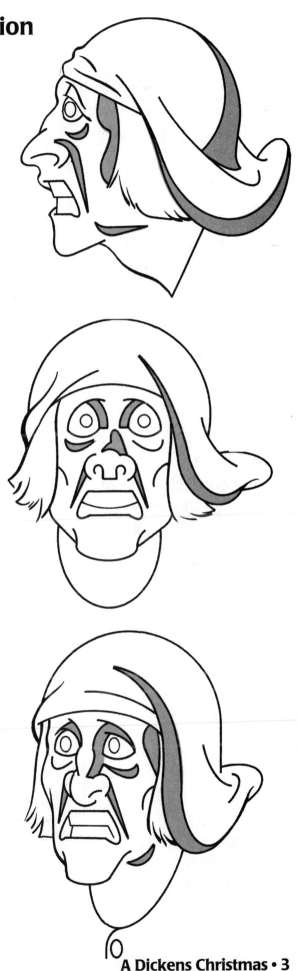

Bulging eyes, flaring nostrils, clenched teeth, wide open turned down mouth are all the features we want in this face to show the fear that Scrooge is experiencing as he looks upon the spirits.

Study the shading on each of the different positions of the face. It will help you understand the peaks and valleys of the contours of the face.

When the carving is completed, sandpaper fairly smooth for a sculptured look. We are going for realism, not caricature. Also the sanding will refine and sharpen the features. Use medium to fine sandpaper.

Suggested Tools:
Knife for general shaping
V-parting tool for cheek lines coming off the nostrils to the bottom of the mouth and for bags under the eyes
Small half round gouge to hollow out over the eyes and along the side of the nose
Veiner for hair detail

Scrooge
Color Program

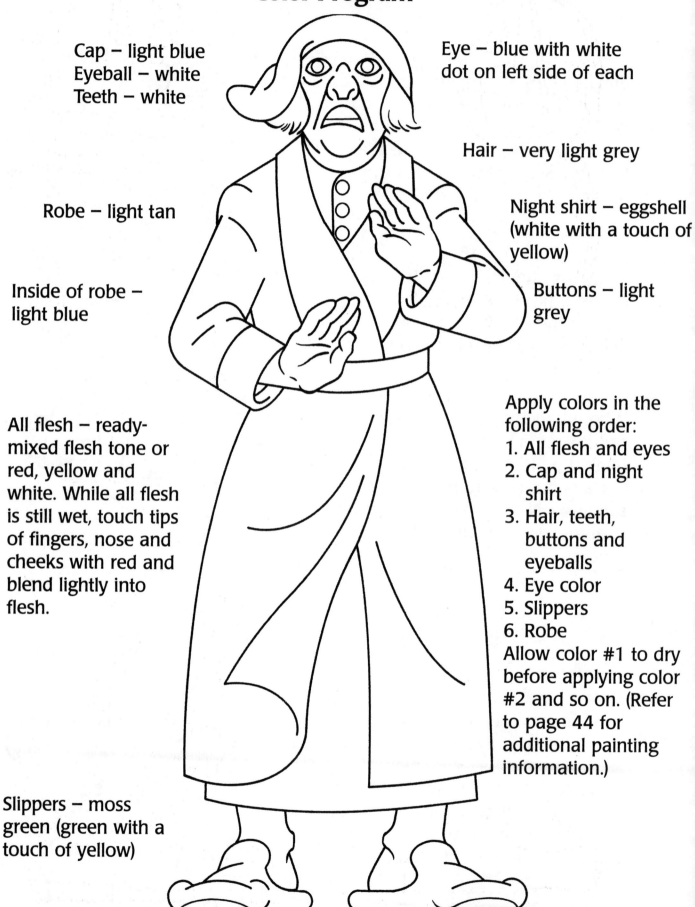

Cap – light blue
Eyeball – white
Teeth – white

Eye – blue with white dot on left side of each

Hair – very light grey

Robe – light tan

Night shirt – eggshell (white with a touch of yellow)

Inside of robe – light blue

Buttons – light grey

All flesh – ready-mixed flesh tone or red, yellow and white. While all flesh is still wet, touch tips of fingers, nose and cheeks with red and blend lightly into flesh.

Apply colors in the following order:
1. All flesh and eyes
2. Cap and night shirt
3. Hair, teeth, buttons and eyeballs
4. Eye color
5. Slippers
6. Robe
Allow color #1 to dry before applying color #2 and so on. (Refer to page 44 for additional painting information.)

Slippers – moss green (green with a touch of yellow)

Marley's Ghost
Side View Patterns

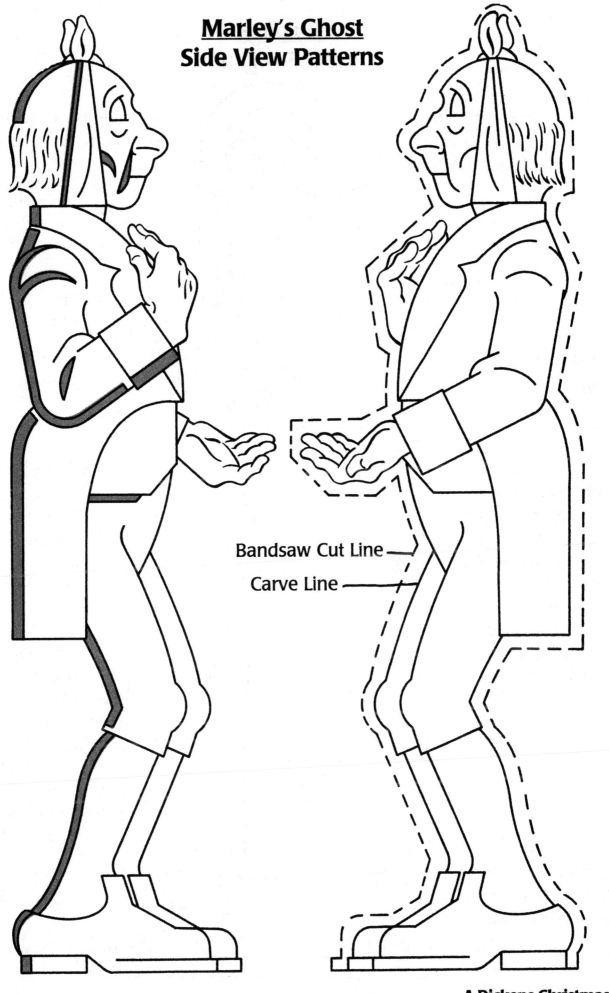

Bandsaw Cut Line

Carve Line

Marley's Ghost
Facial Expression

"Marley was dead, to begin with."
These famous opening lines of the classic tell us exactly where we want to go in carving this face. The cloth wrapped around the head to keep the jaw from dropping open, the closed eyes, hollow cheeks and general expressionless attitude.

Study the shading on each of the different positions of the face to understand the modeling we want to achieve.

When the carving is complete, sandpaper fairly smooth for the sculptured realism we want.

Suggested Tools:
Knife for general shaping
V-parting tool for the nose and the
   lines coming from nose to the
   mouth also for the detail of the
   cloth around the head
Half round gouge to hollow out
   over the eyes and shaping of
   the nose
Veiner for hair detail

Marley's Ghost
Color Program

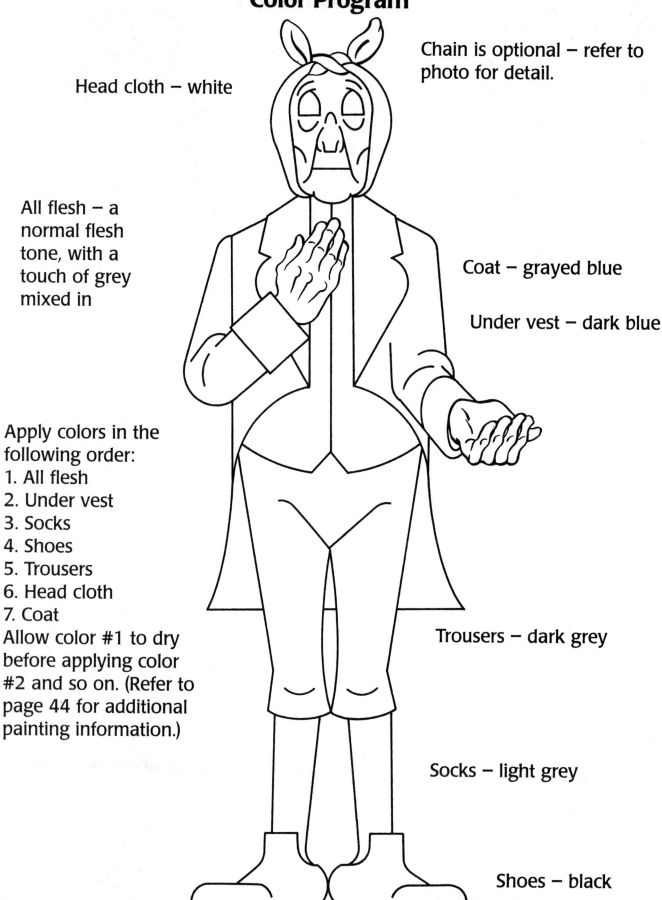

Head cloth – white

Chain is optional – refer to photo for detail.

All flesh – a normal flesh tone, with a touch of grey mixed in

Coat – grayed blue

Under vest – dark blue

Apply colors in the following order:
1. All flesh
2. Under vest
3. Socks
4. Shoes
5. Trousers
6. Head cloth
7. Coat

Allow color #1 to dry before applying color #2 and so on. (Refer to page 44 for additional painting information.)

Trousers – dark grey

Socks – light grey

Shoes – black

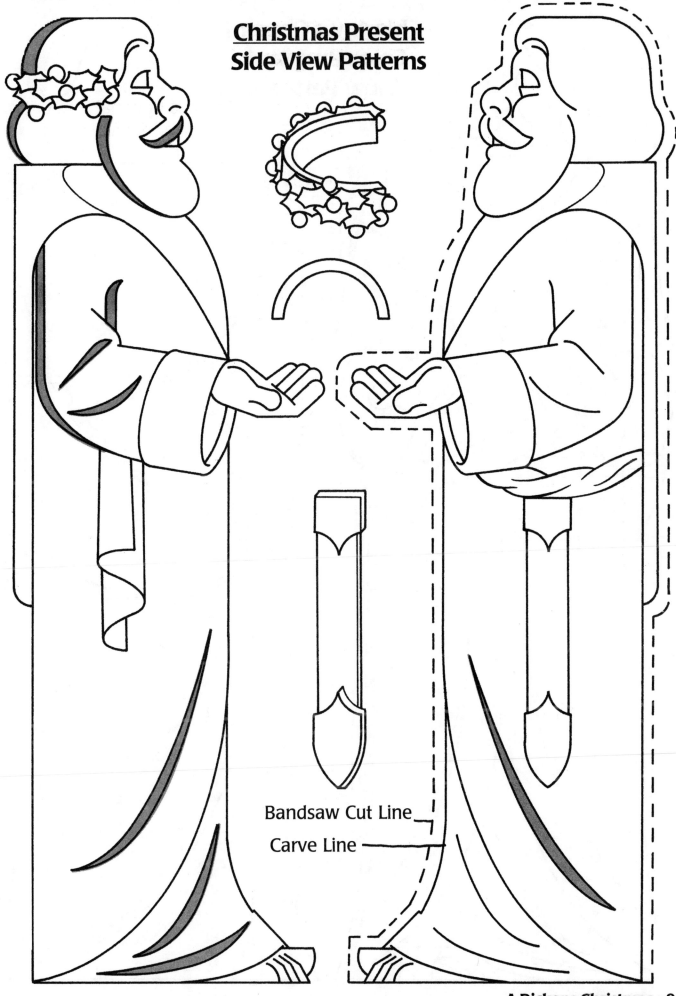

Christmas Present
Side View Patterns

Bandsaw Cut Line

Carve Line

Christmas Present
Front and Back
View Patterns

Christmas Present
Facial Expression

In this face there must be all the majesty and wonder that is Christmas, along with the joy and peace it represents. The face should be round, abundant, kind, and yes, merry.

Study the shading to help guide you in carving. Go to the sandpaper for finish. The wreath is optional. It can be carved as part of the hair arrangement or carved separately and added on. (Refer to page 9 for detail.)

Suggested Tools:
The veiner and knife work well on this piece.

The horn of plenty is optional. It is carved from a solid block. The fruit is ready-made wood balls. Hollow out the front end slightly as shown to receive the fruit. (Refer to the photo of Christmas Present for placement.)

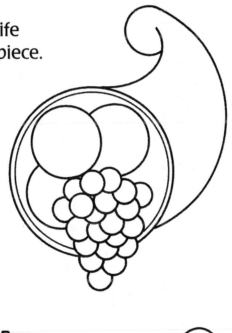

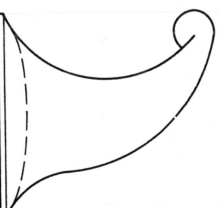

Christmas Present
Color Program

Hair and beard –
bright orange

Eyeball – white

Eyes – light brown with
white dot on left side of
each

Robe – emerald
green

Under garment –
eggshell

Fur collar – white

All flesh and
eyes – normal
flesh tone. While
flesh color is still
wet, blend in a
touch of red to
cheeks and
lower lip.

Waist sash –
vermillion

Scabbard – white with
gold trim

Apply colors in the
following order:
1. All flesh
2. Under garment
3. Fur collar
4. Robe
5. Waist sash
6. Scabbard

If horn of plenty is to
be added, paint
separately and attach.
Horn is gold, color fruit
accordingly. (Refer to
photo.)

Tiny Tim
Side View Patterns

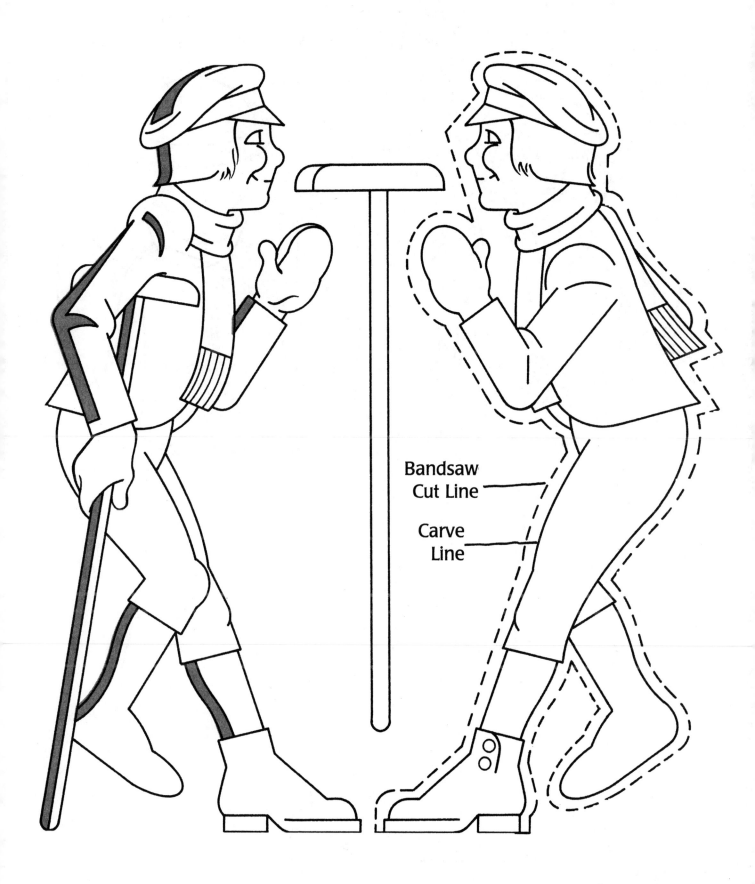

Bandsaw
Cut Line

Carve
Line

Tiny Tim
Front and Back View Patterns

Tiny Tim
Facial Expression

In Tiny Ti_____ _____ of
Christma_____
little bo_____
rises ab_____
wonde_____
right.

_____t in this
_____of this
_____t to

Sugg_____
Knife _____
Half rou_____ gouge for
   detailing
V-parting tool to separate side hair line
   from cheeks
Veiner to complete hair detail
Sandpaper to finish

Tiny Tim
Color Program

All flesh − normal flesh tone with touch of white to lighten. While flesh color is still wet touch cheeks and lip with red and blend.

Cap − dark brown

Hair − yellow brown

Eyeball − white

Eyes − blue with white dot on each side

Scarf − vermillion

Jacket − dark blue grey

Mittens − vermillion

Trousers − charcoal brown

Socks − light blue grey

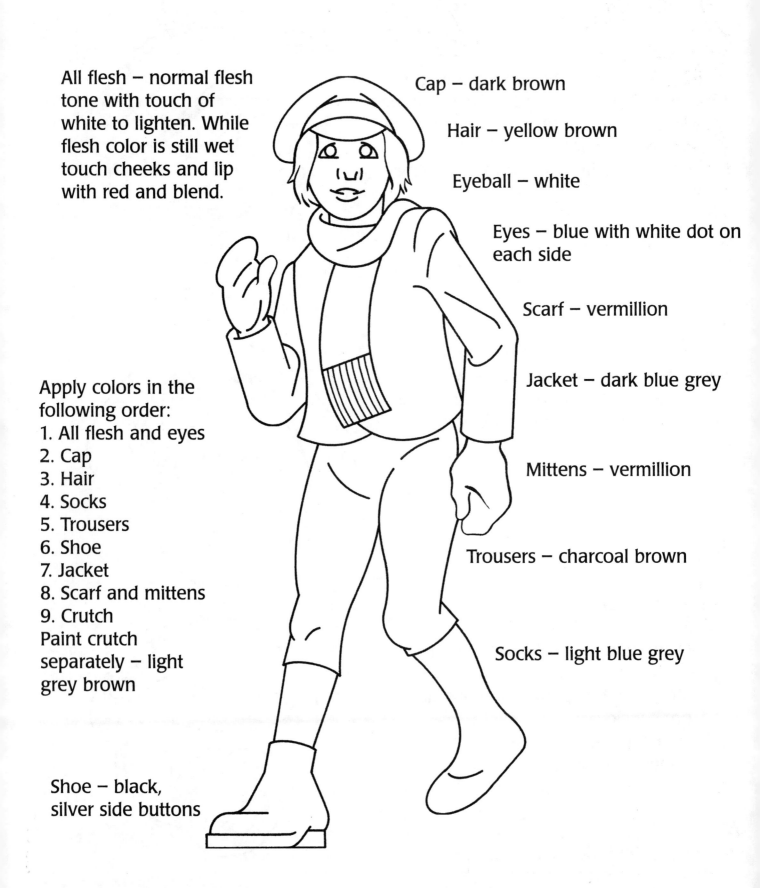

Apply colors in the following order:
1. All flesh and eyes
2. Cap
3. Hair
4. Socks
5. Trousers
6. Shoe
7. Jacket
8. Scarf and mittens
9. Crutch
Paint crutch separately − light grey brown

Shoe − black, silver side buttons

Bob Cratchit
Side View Patterns

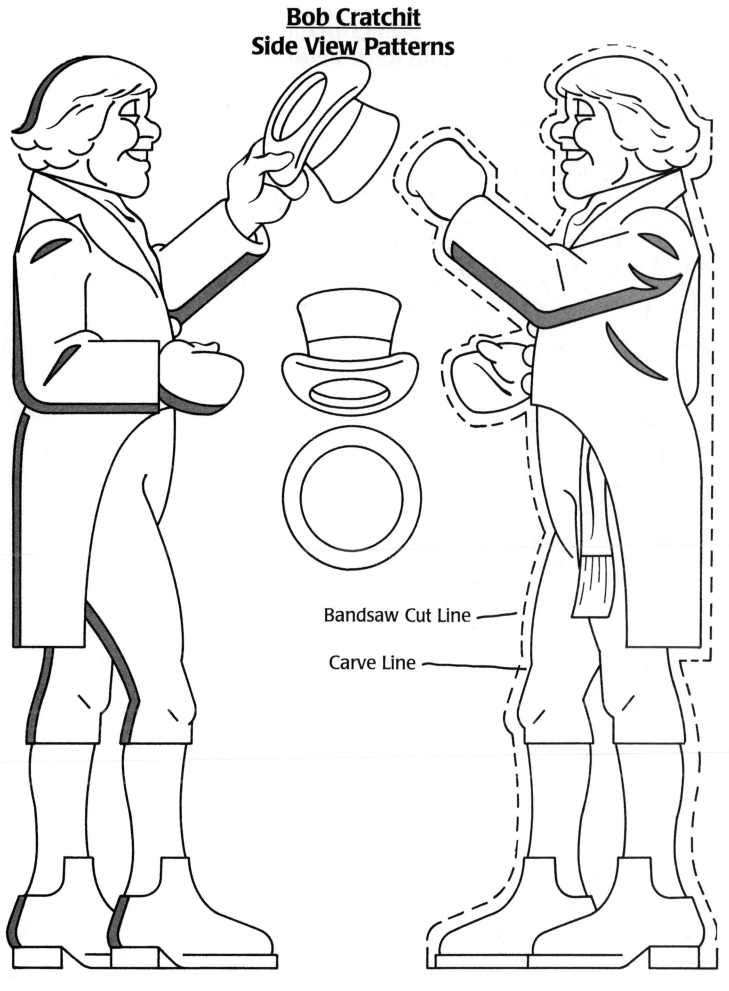

Bandsaw Cut Line

Carve Line

Bob Cratchit
Front and Back View Patterns

Bob Cratchit
Facial Expression

Overworked, underpayed, constantly harassed by Scrooge... This is what Bob Cratchit has to endure. But with it all, he continues on. Faithful to his family, hardworking and trustworthy, truly Bob Cratchit is a man of goodwill and cheer.

Study the shading for a better understanding of the face anatomy. We are going for a strong happy face, but with traces of life's hardships upon it also.

Suggested Tools:
Knife for general shaping
Small half round gouge for side of nose and cheeks, also for over the eyes
V-parting tool to enhance side hair line from cheek
Veiner for fine detail of hair
Finish with sandpaper

Bob Cratchit
Color Program

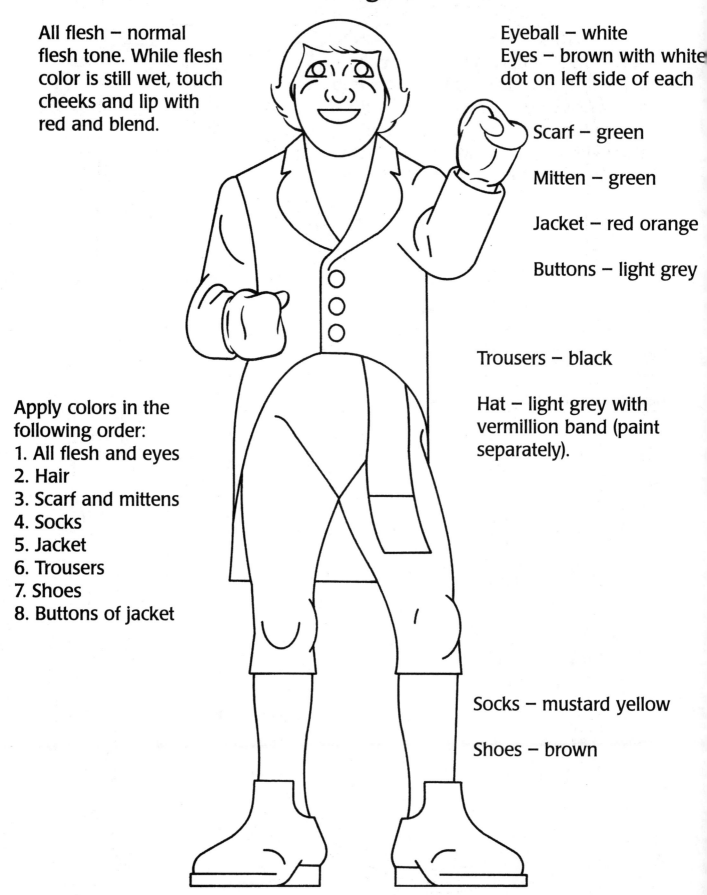

All flesh – normal flesh tone. While flesh color is still wet, touch cheeks and lip with red and blend.

Eyeball – white
Eyes – brown with white dot on left side of each

Scarf – green

Mitten – green

Jacket – red orange

Buttons – light grey

Trousers – black

Hat – light grey with vermillion band (paint separately).

Apply colors in the following order:
1. All flesh and eyes
2. Hair
3. Scarf and mittens
4. Socks
5. Jacket
6. Trousers
7. Shoes
8. Buttons of jacket

Socks – mustard yellow

Shoes – brown

Base Pattern

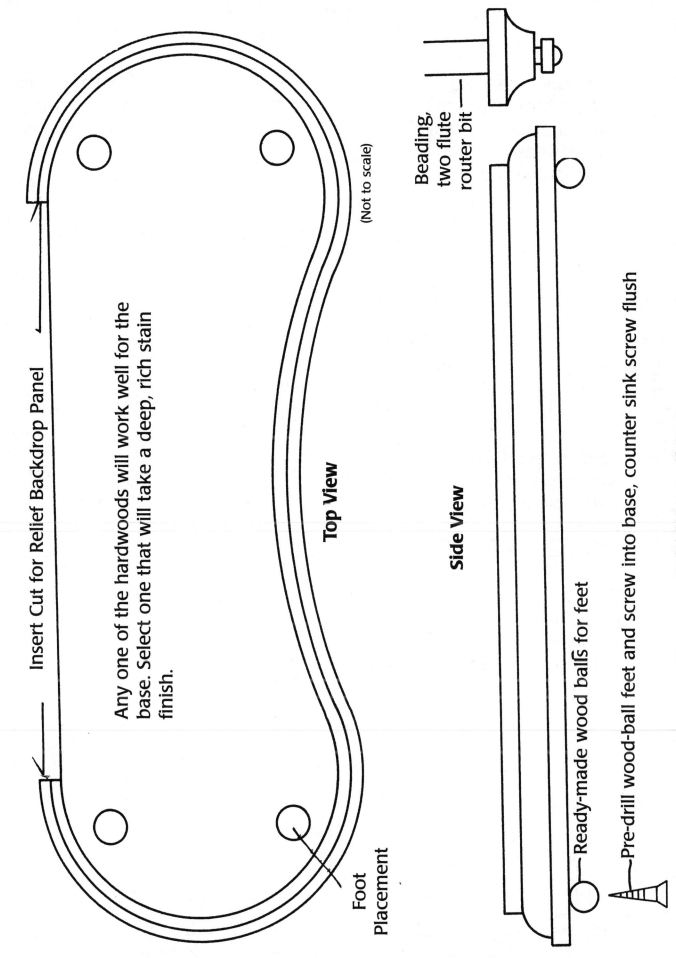

Insert Cut for Relief Backdrop Panel

Any one of the hardwoods will work well for the base. Select one that will take a deep, rich stain finish.

Top View

(Not to scale)

Side View

Foot Placement

Beading, two flute router bit

Ready-made wood balls for feet

Pre-drill wood-ball feet and screw into base, counter sink screw flush

Relief Backdrop Pattern

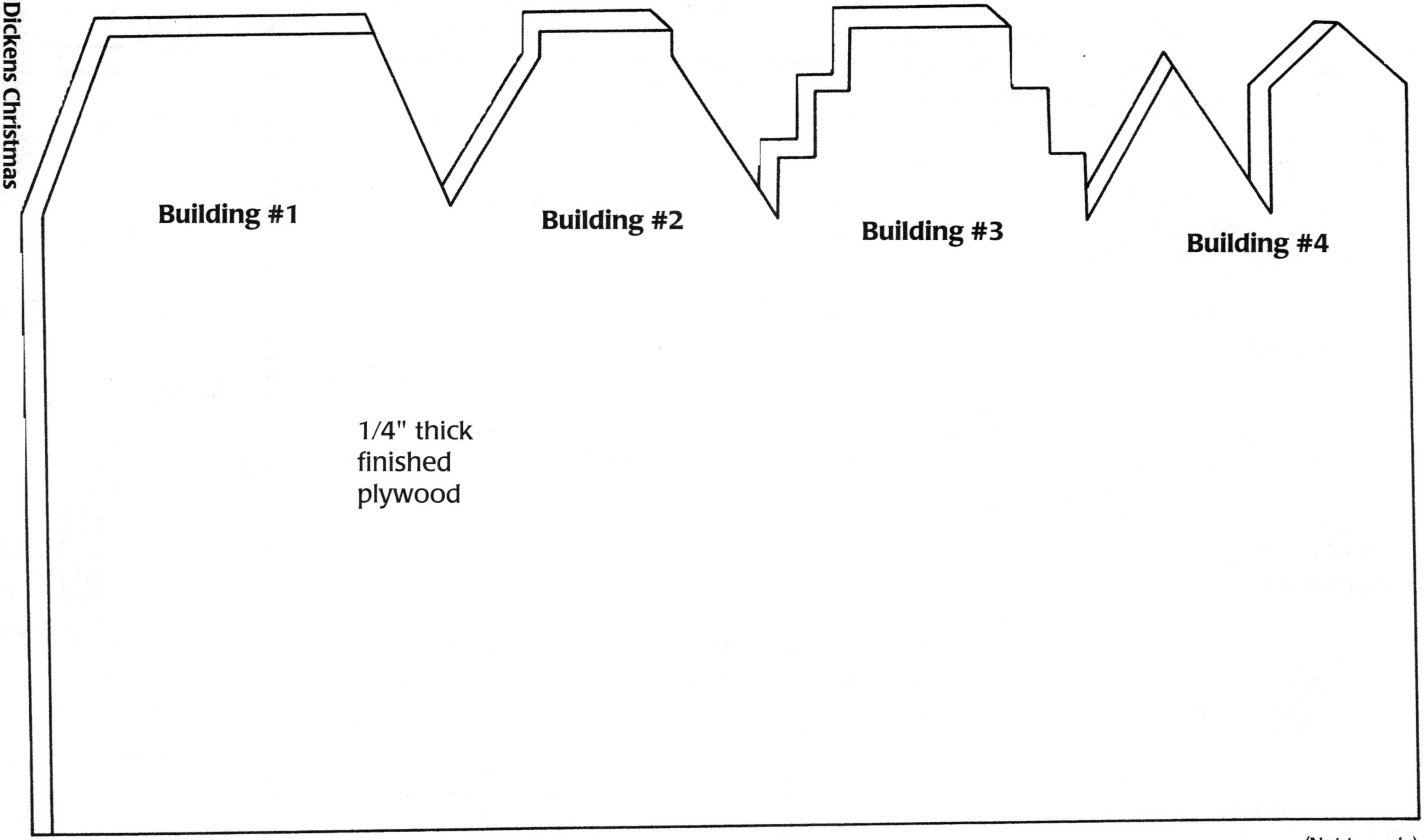

Building #1

Building #2

Building #3

Building #4

1/4" thick
finished
plywood

(Not to scale)

Detail of Fitting Relief Backdrop Panel to Base

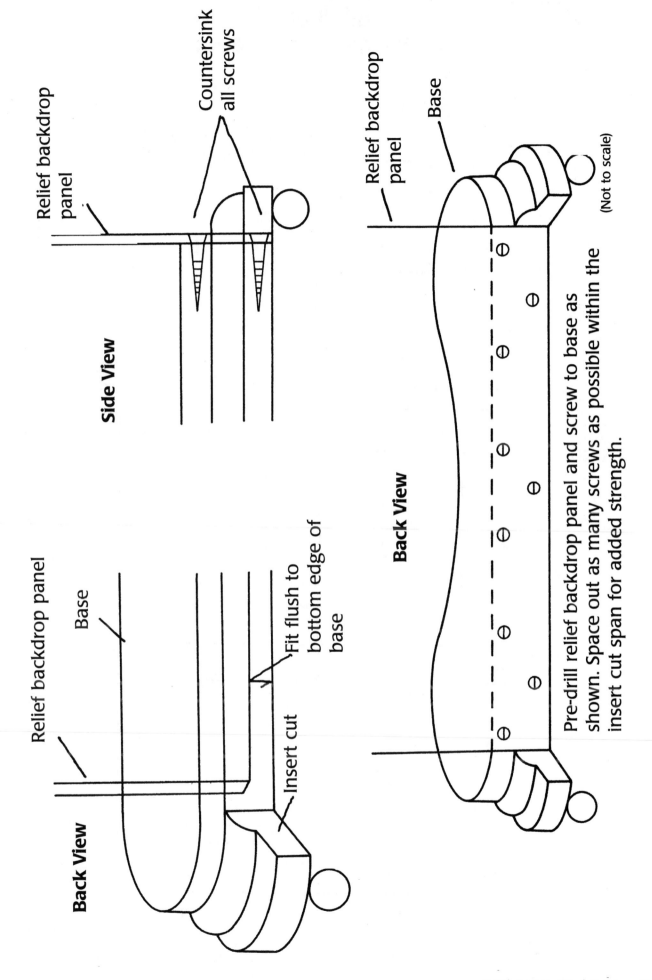

Side View

Relief backdrop panel

Countersink all screws

Back View

Relief backdrop panel

Base

Fit flush to bottom edge of base

Insert cut

Back View

Relief backdrop panel

Base

(Not to scale)

Pre-drill relief backdrop panel and screw to base as shown. Space out as many screws as possible within the insert cut span for added strength.

Building #1
Pattern, Front Elevation

Basswood sheets 1/8" thick are ideal for the built-up relief effect.

(Not to scale)

Building #1
Detail of Relief Effect

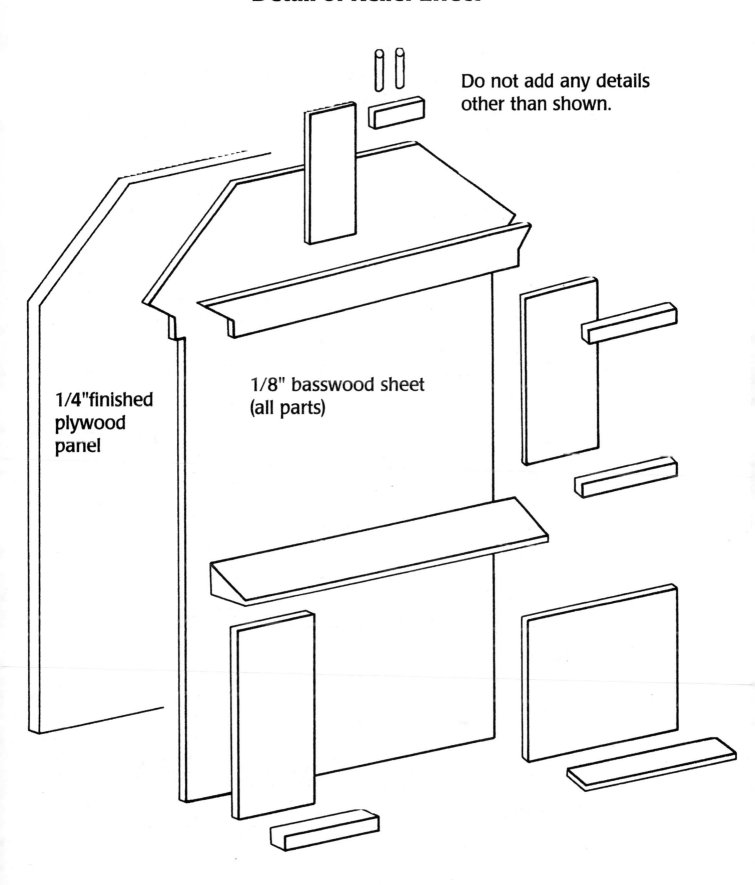

Do not add any details other than shown.

1/4"finished plywood panel

1/8" basswood sheet (all parts)

Building #1
Color Program

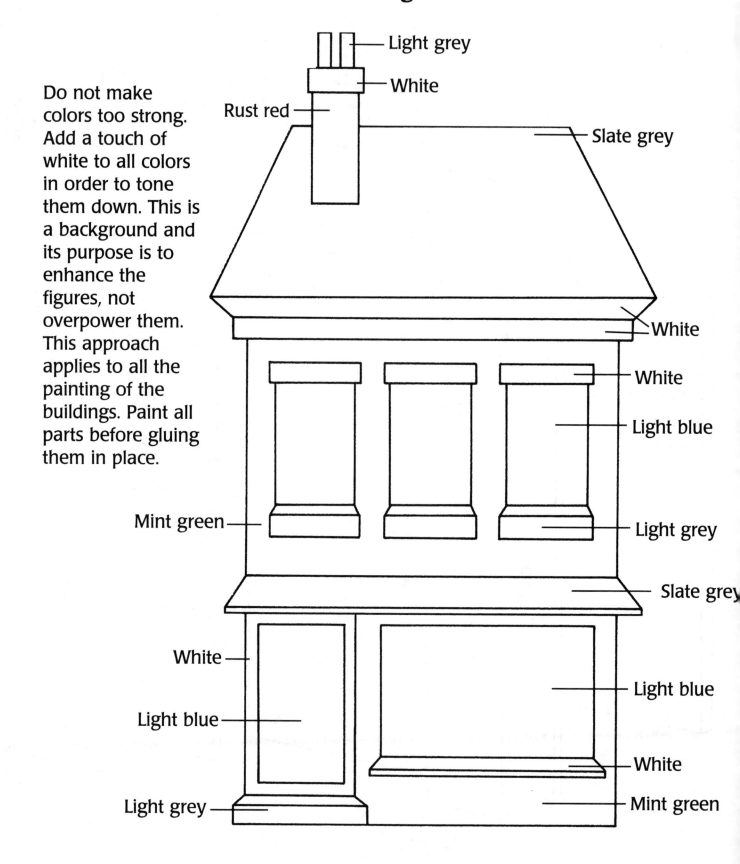

Do not make colors too strong. Add a touch of white to all colors in order to tone them down. This is a background and its purpose is to enhance the figures, not overpower them. This approach applies to all the painting of the buildings. Paint all parts before gluing them in place.

Light grey

White

Rust red

Slate grey

White

White

Light blue

Mint green

Light grey

Slate grey

White

Light blue

Light blue

White

Light grey

Mint green

Building #2
Pattern, Front Elevation

(Not to scale)

Building #2
Detail of Relief Effect

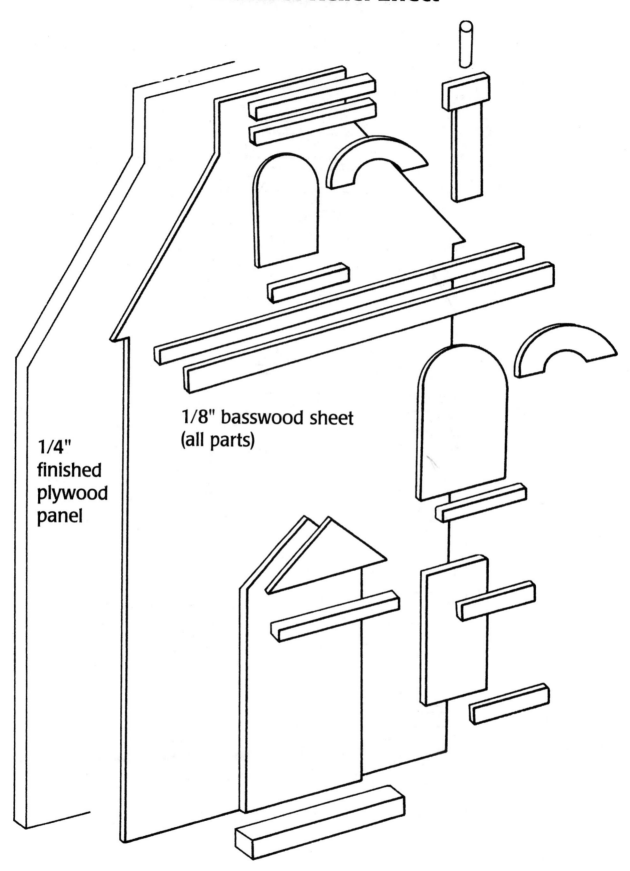

1/4"
finished
plywood
panel

1/8" basswood sheet
(all parts)

Building #2
Color Program

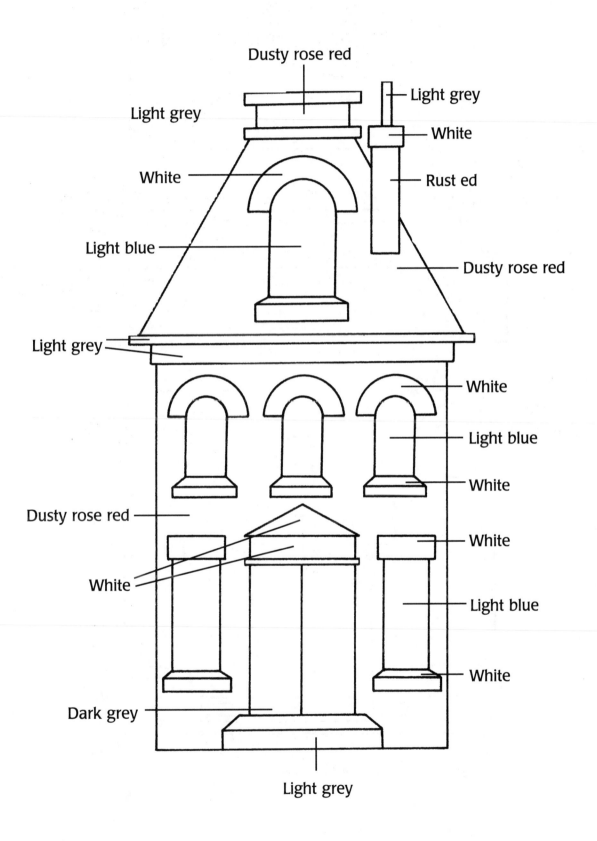

Dusty rose red

Light grey

Light grey

White

White

Rust ed

Light blue

Dusty rose red

Light grey

White

Light blue

White

Dusty rose red

White

White

Light blue

White

Dark grey

Light grey

Building #3
Pattern, Front Elevation

(Not to scale)

Building #3
Detail of Relief Effect

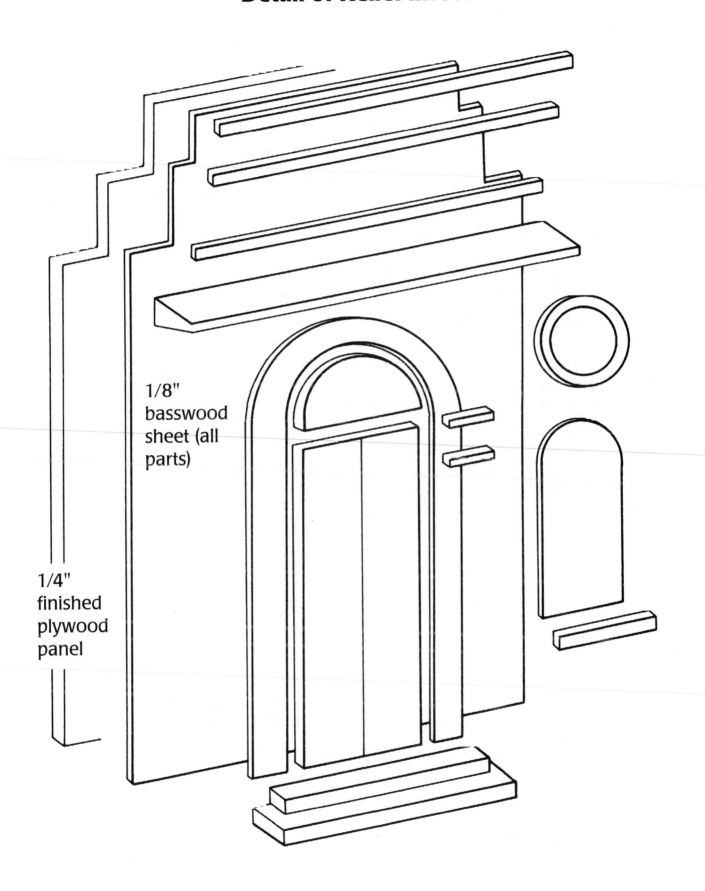

1/8" basswood sheet (all parts)

1/4" finished plywood panel

Building #3
Color Program

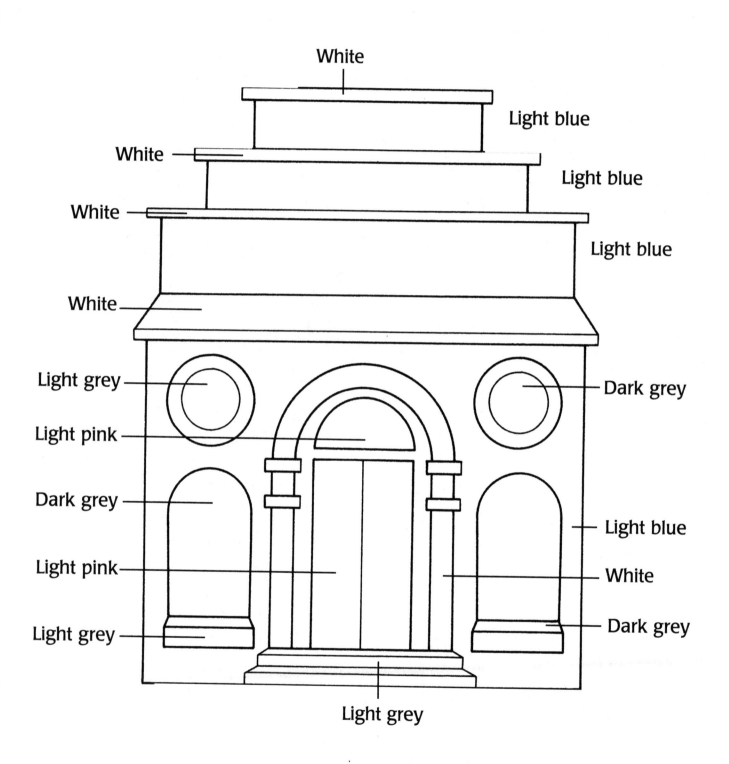

White

Light blue

White

Light blue

White

Light blue

White

Light grey

Dark grey

Light pink

Dark grey

Light blue

Light pink

White

Light grey

Dark grey

Light grey

Building #4
Pattern, Front Elevation

(Not to scale)

Building #4
Detail of Relief Effect

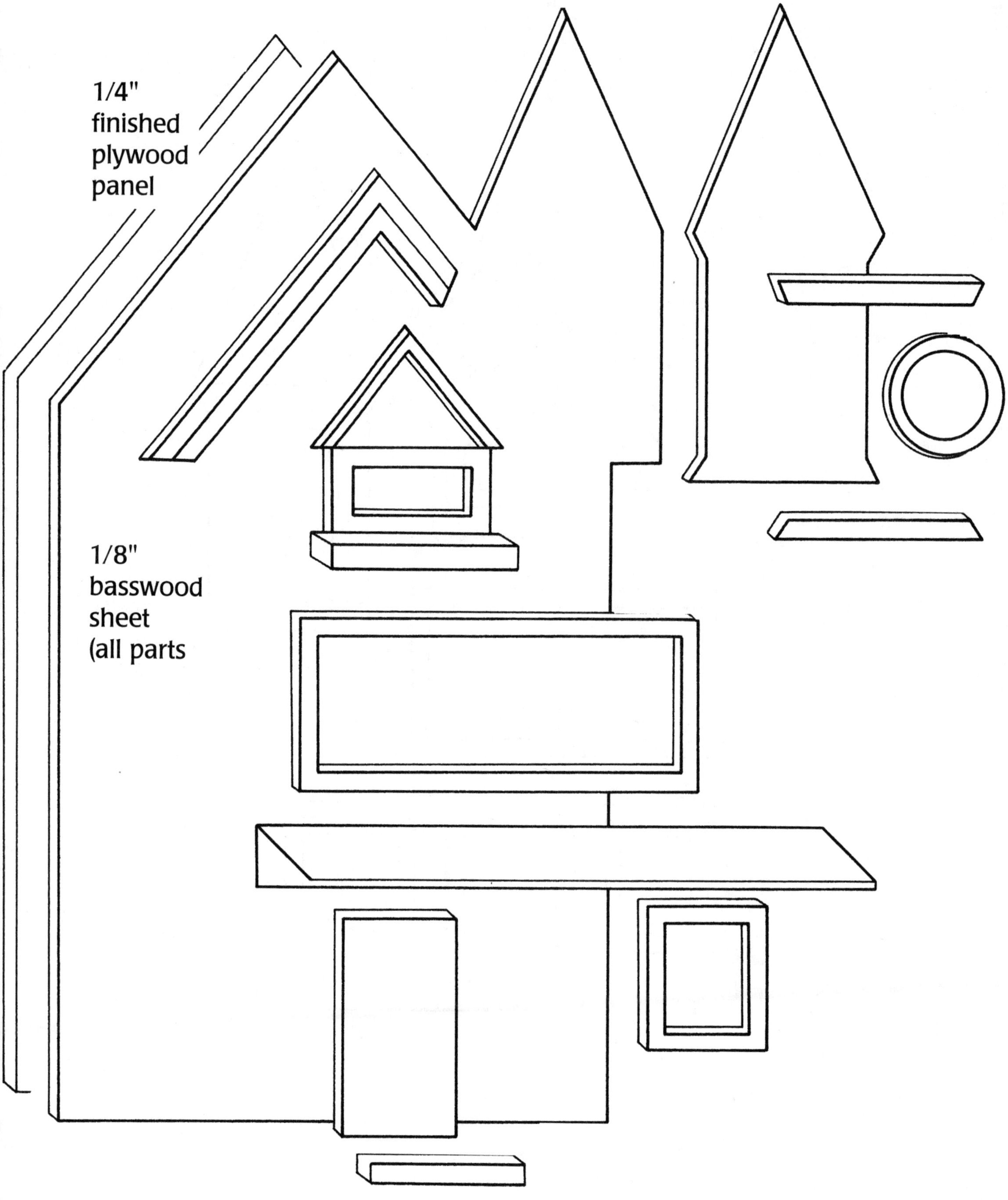

1/4"
finished
plywood
panel

1/8"
basswood
sheet
(all parts

Building #4
Color Program

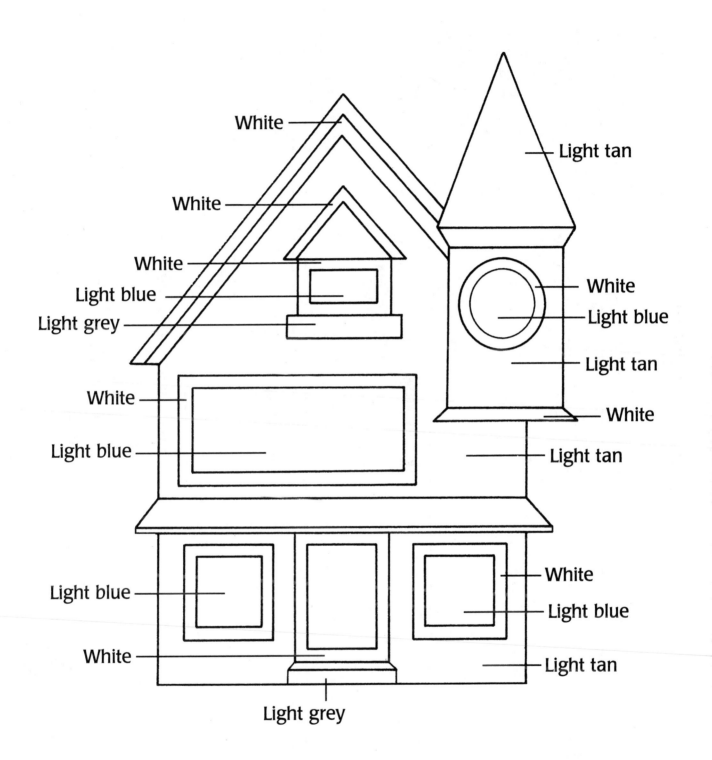

White

White

White

Light blue

Light grey

White

Light blue

Light blue

White

Light grey

Light tan

White

Light blue

Light tan

White

Light tan

White

Light blue

Light tan

Name Plate Pattern

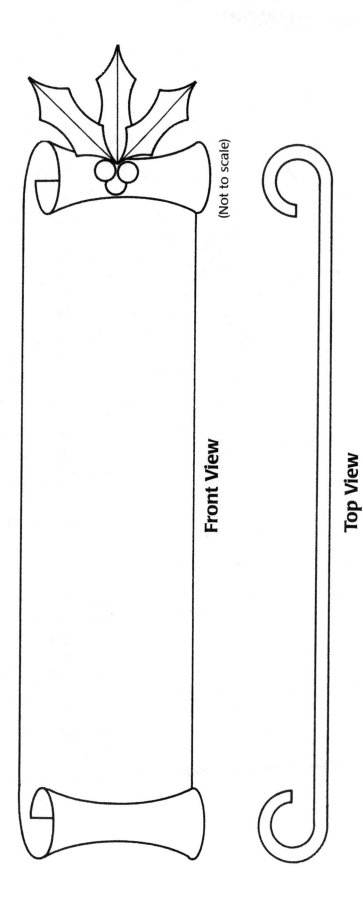

Front View

(Not to scale)

Top View

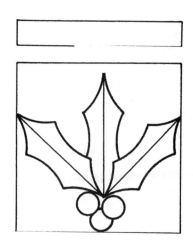

Carve holly leaves separately. Berries are ready-made wood balls. Paint holly leaves and berries before mounting to end of name plate. A detail knife works well for the carving of the holly leaves.

Name Plate
Carving Tips

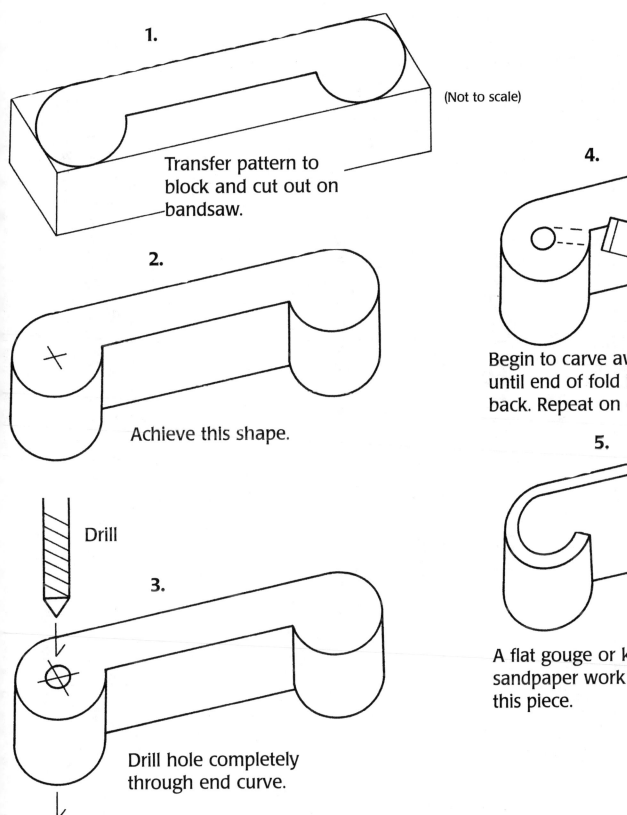

1.

(Not to scale)

Transfer pattern to block and cut out on bandsaw.

2.

Achieve this shape.

Drill

3.

Drill hole completely through end curve.

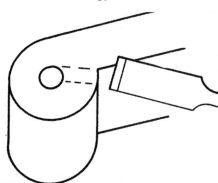

4.

Begin to carve away excess until end of fold is free from back. Repeat on other end.

5.

A flat gouge or knife and sandpaper work well for this piece.

Name Plate Color Program and Lettering Guide

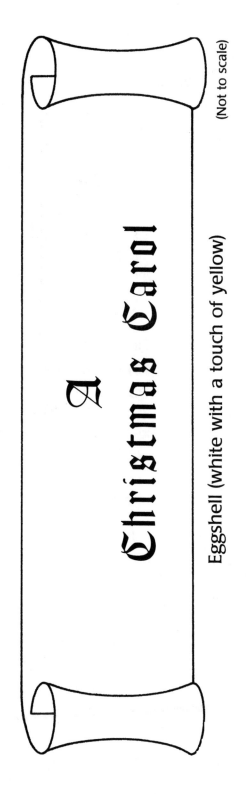

(Not to scale)

A
Christmas Carol

Eggshell (white with a touch of yellow)

Moss Green (green with a touch of yellow)

Gently outline edge of holly leaves with yellow

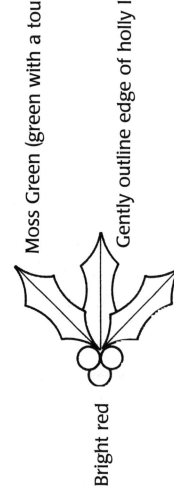

Bright red

Vinyl plastic peel and stick-on letters usually can be found at art supply or stationery stores. The name of this style is "Old English Text" typeface. The size of the lettering will be determined by the size you decide to make the name plate. Carefully space out the words "A Christmas Carol" before final application. Finish all painting and spraying before applying lettering. The color of the lettering could be black, red or green.

Decorative End Brace

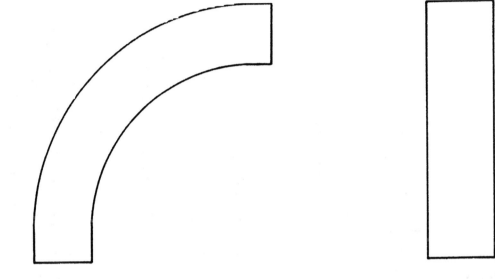

Side View
(without holly leaves)

Front View
(without holly leaves)

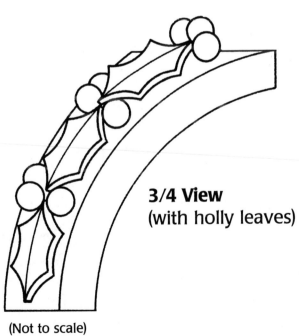

3/4 View
(with holly leaves)

(Not to scale)

Decorative End Brace Pattern

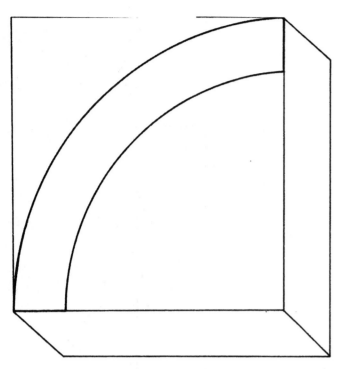

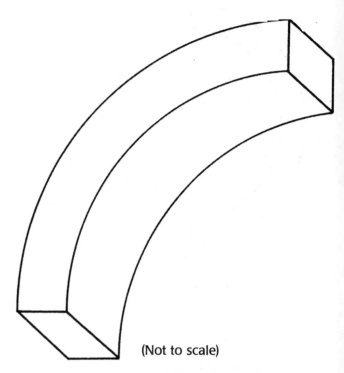

(Not to scale)

Transfer pattern to block and cut out on bandsaw.

Two of this shape are required. (Same)

Holly Leaves Pattern

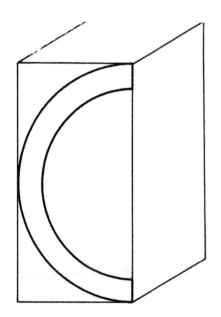

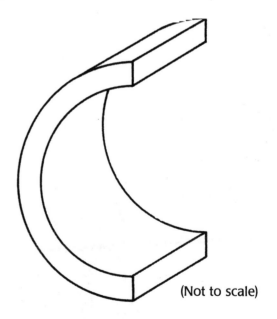

(Not to scale)

Transfer pattern to block and cut out on bandsaw.

Six of this shape are required. (Same)

Decorative End Brace
Carving the Holly Leaves and Assembly

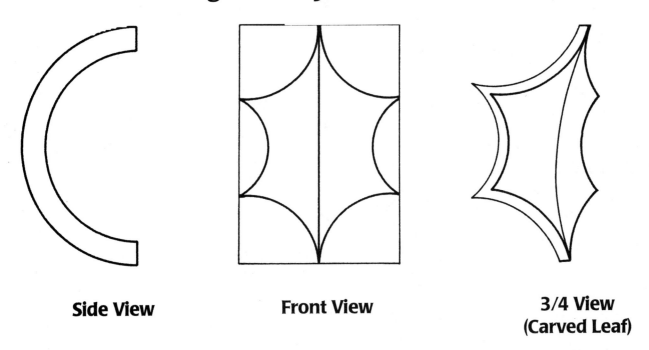

Side View

Front View

**3/4 View
(Carved Leaf)**

Use knife and sandpaper to complete each leaf. Be careful to maintain the curve of the leaf so it will march the curve of the brace.

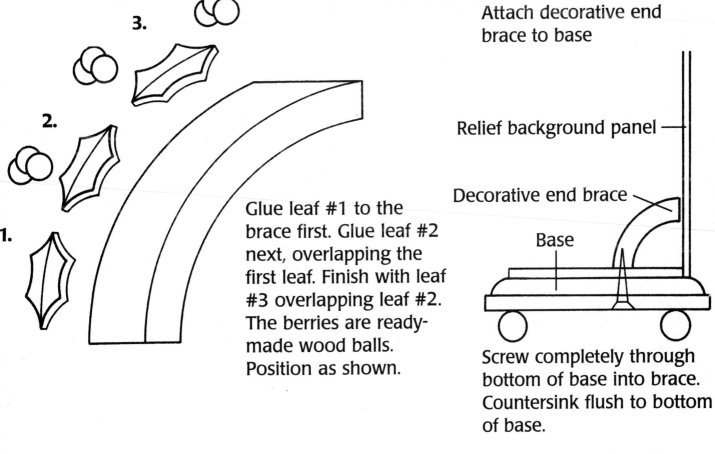

Glue leaf #1 to the brace first. Glue leaf #2 next, overlapping the first leaf. Finish with leaf #3 overlapping leaf #2. The berries are ready-made wood balls. Position as shown.

Attach decorative end brace to base

Relief background panel

Decorative end brace

Base

Screw completely through bottom of base into brace. Countersink flush to bottom of base.

Decorative End Brace
Color Program

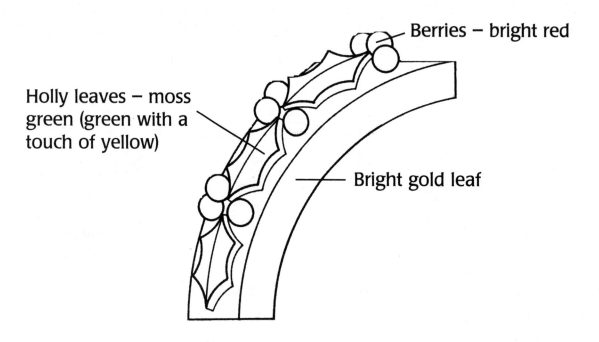

Berries – bright red

Holly leaves – moss green (green with a touch of yellow)

Bright gold leaf

Apply gold leaf to brace first. Paint holly leaves and berries separately. Let dry. Apply protective spray. Let dry. Do not apply protective spray to gold leaf. It may affect the finish. Screw brace only to base then finish by gluing holly leaves and berries in place.

Position decorative end brace at slight angle as shown.

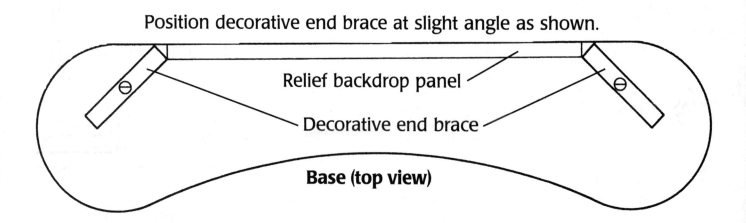

Relief backdrop panel

Decorative end brace

Base (top view)

Attaching and Arranging Figures on Base

All figures are drilled, doweled and glued to base. All drilling and fitting of dowels should be completed before gluing and painting.

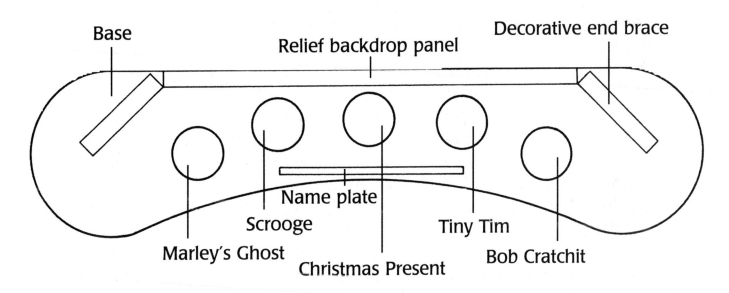

Base

Relief backdrop panel

Decorative end brace

Name plate

Scrooge

Marley's Ghost

Christmas Present

Tiny Tim

Bob Cratchit

Arrange all figures on base and mark base for drilling of placement of dowels to base.

One dowel per figure is sufficient. Also complete all drilling in figures and base. Then arrange everything for proper fit before gluing.

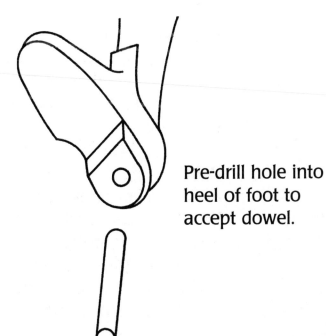

Pre-drill hole into heel of foot to accept dowel.

Painting Tips, Brushes and Paints

The quality of the paint and brushes you select to finish this project is very important, for all the hours you invested in carving the project can quickly be lost by an inferior paint job. The same attention must be paid to fine brushes and paint as to fine cutting tools. Both make the art of carving and finishing wood more enjoyable and rewarding.

Color is crucial to this project because they enhance the mood of the characters more strongly along with the facial expressions and body attitudes. For example, look at the cold color scheme of Marley's Ghost contrasted to the warm, gay color scheme of Bob Cratchit. Both immediately tell you who and what they are. One is without life while the other is full of life. This is the mind set you want in approaching all of the characters as far as painting them.

Use some type of mounting device, such as a paint stick, to minimize handling of the piece during the painting process. Never paint a light color over a dark color; so it's a good idea to paint all of the light shades first, allowing them to dry thoroughly, then apply all darker shades. The secret to a professional paint job is neatness first, cutting or overlapping one color over the other in a clean consistent line. So always go a bit farther with the first applied color so when you come in with the second overlapping color you can cut it sharply.

Try not to make your colors too intense, but rather go for more pastel shade. Pastel shades can be made simply by adding a touch of white to any color. They give a softer look as opposed to colors used straight out of a tube or jar. Finally the best advice I can give is to work carefully, think first, then apply paint. Allow a two-day drying time on all completed pieces before applying a protective spray.

Brushes
The large soft-hair fan brush is for all large body areas. The small round soft-hair brush is for all detail work. It's a good idea to have a few of each brush.

Paint
Acrylic—Water-based, good for all large flat areas. Will not blend. Will mix with other colors. Soap and water clean up.

Alkyd—Oil-based, good for all skin tones and hair. Will blend to achieve shading. Will mix with other colors. Spirits of turpentine clean up.

About the Author

Vince Squeglia is a commercial artist with over thirty-five years experience in all media. His work has been published in the United States and Europe. As Art Director for the Greenpoint Cultural Society of New York City, he taught representational drawing and painting (portraiture and human anatomy). He has had numerous one-man shows both selling and exhibition. Vince began wood carving about a year and a half ago as a way to unwind from his busy New York studio schedule.

Facial expression and body attitude are first considerations in Vince's creations, followed by fine clear detailing and finishing in custom-mixed colors applied in clean cut lines. These are the elements that bring forth the character of the piece and give it life. This approach is most evident in the theme of this book.

All of Vince's original pattern portfolios are available by contacting Vince at 58 Conselyea Street, Brooklyn, New York, 11211.

You are invited to Join the

National Wood Carvers Association
"Some carve their careers: others just chisel"
since 1953

If you have any interest in woodcarving: if you carve wood, create wood sculpture or even just whittle in your spare time, you will enjoy your membership in the National Wood Carvers Association. The non-profit NWCA is the world's largest carving club with over 33,000 members. There are NWCA members in more than 56 countries around the globe.

The Association's goals are to:
- promote wood carving
- foster fellowship among member enthusiasts
- encourage exhibitions and area get togethers
- list sources of equipment and information for the wood carving artist
- provide a forum for carving artists

The NWCA serves as a valuable network of tips, hints and helpful information for the wood carver. Membership is only $11.00 per year.

Members receive the magazine "Chip Chats" six times a year, free with their membership. "Chip Chats" contains articles, news events, demonstrations of technique, patterns and a full color section showcasing examples of fine craftsmanship. Through this magazine you will be kept up to date on shows and workshops to attend, new products, special offers to NWCA members and other members' activities in your area and around the world.

National Wood Carvers Association
7424 Miami Ave.
Cincinnati, OH 45243

Name: _____

Address: _____

_____

Dues $11.00 per year in USA, $14.00 per year foreign (payable in US Funds)

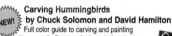

NEW AND RECENT BOOK TITLES...
...from the experts!

Making Classic Chairs:
A Craftsman's Chippendale Reference
Ron Clarkson & Tom Heller

188 pp. softcover
1-56523-081-7   **$24.95**

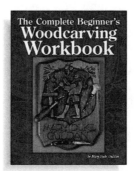

Complete Beginner's Woodcarving Workbook
Mary Duke Guldan

Softcover, 56 pages, 8.5 x 11
1-56523-085-X $9.95

Carousel Horse Carving:
An Instructional Workbook in 1/3 scale
Ken Hughes

Perfect bound, color and black and white,
how-to information, tool lists, full size
pattern included.
1-56523-072-8 $24.95

East Weekend Carving Projects
Tina Toney

56 pp. perfect bound, color and black and
white, step-by-step carving and painting
demonstrations patterns.
1-56523-084-1 $12.95

Santas and Snowmen:
Carving for Christmas
Tina Toney

56 pp. softcover, Full color.
1-56523-083-3 $12.95

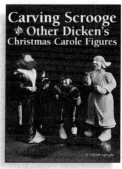

**Carving Scrooge and Dickens's
"A Christmas Carol"**
(plus the Olde London Towne scene)
Vince Squeglia

56 pp. 10 complete patterns,
full color gallery included.
1-56523-082-5 $12.95

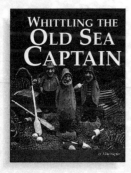

Whittling the Old Sea Captain
Mike Shipley

48 pp. perfect bound, color and black and
white. Includes step-by-step carving &
painting demonstrations, patterns, color
photos of the finished captain crew.
1-56523-075-2 $12.95

Free Form Chip Carving
Carol A. Ponte

48 pp. softcover
1-56523-080-9 $7.95

Santa Carving With Myron Bowman

56 pp. perfect bound, color and black and
white. Includes step-by-step carving and
painting demonstrations, 11 patterns, color
photos of finished Santas.
1-56523-076-0 $12.95

FOX BOOKS
Fox Chapel Publishing Co. Inc.

Fox Chapel Publishing Co., Inc.
PO Box 7948
Lancaster, PA 17604-7948

Ordering Information:
Try your favorite book supplier first!
Or see information on following pages to order direct from the publisher.